DELLA TEMPLE

Tame Your Inner Critic

The Workbook

A Companion Workbook for
Living Your Life on Purpose

Tame Your Inner Critic The Workbook
Della Temple

Cover and Interior Design: Rebecca Finkel, F+P Graphic Design
Illustrations: Shannon Parish, Illustrating You.
Publisher: Button Rock Press, 942 Spruce Drive Lyons, CO 80540

ISBN: 978-0-692-28404-9

Categories for cataloging and shelving:
1. Self-Help   2. Spiritual

Printed in the USA

Contents

Introduction

You are about to undertake a truly amazing process. Taming your inner critic is deep, soulful work, but it is not always easy. You may shed tears as you work with some of the deeper stories of judgment, shame, and external criticism. You may laugh as you uncover hidden truths and banish the energy of "should." Above all, you will learn how to curb the loud, persistent chatter of your inner critic, replacing it with the voice of your inner guidance, your Spirit. As you do so, your inner world will become a place of stillness and peace. Here you will come in contact with the part of yourself that is connected to the Divine.

How to Use This Workbook

Taming your inner critic and uncovering your life's purpose is both a left-brain and a right-brain activity. Sometimes it's important to follow the directions and do the exercises as described in the book. Other times you will be drawn to journal, to doodle, or to describe your process through free-form writing. This workbook has space for you to do both. It is your diary, your journal, your best friend, and a lifeline to your own internal wisdom.

Interspersed among the suggested exercises and meditations are a few thought-provoking questions, urging you to dig deep into the recesses of your own internal wisdom.

As you work through the chapters of *Tame Your Inner Critic*, you will learn to fill yourself with your own true power, finding peace and contentment as you discover the gift you are meant to share with the world. This companion workbook gives you a forum for finding your own personal path and helps you chart your progress along the way.

Helpful Hints for Your Journey of Discovery

The following suggestions will bring in ease and grace during the process.

- **Set aside a certain time and place,** free from the distractions of your life, to do the daily meditation, exercises, and journaling. The more of your energy you devote to this process, the more you will see success reflected in your life.

- **Be patient.** You've had a lifetime to build up your inner critic's voice, so it might take some time to dismantle it.

- **Bring an attitude of ease and play to the process.** Work and effort are not prerequisites to living the life of your dreams. That's old-school thinking. Understanding the concept that what you think and feel you will be is the new-school way. You really are a magnet attracting events and circumstances into your life that are in alignment with your thoughts and feelings. So think ease, not effort. Think happy and light, not tight and tense. It's all about the be-ing, not the do-ing.

On your journey of discovery, your thoughts, feelings, beliefs, words, and actions will begin to support your life's purpose. That is the joy. That is grace. As you come to know, deep within your soul, that you are living a life full of inner purpose and meaning, you radiate this joy into the world, and that in turn, affects everyone around you.

Let's get started.

CHAPTER 1 # The Energy of "Should"

Big Picture Ideas

- Thoughts are energy—like everything else on this planet. Thoughts travel and are sticky.

- Foreign energy is not bad, just different from our own.

- Our aura is our energetic body.

- The inner critic voice is a mash-up of all the thoughts, feelings, judgments criticisms that other people have sent our way (foreign energy) and we've accepted as our own truth.

Exercise 1.1 Sensing Your Aura

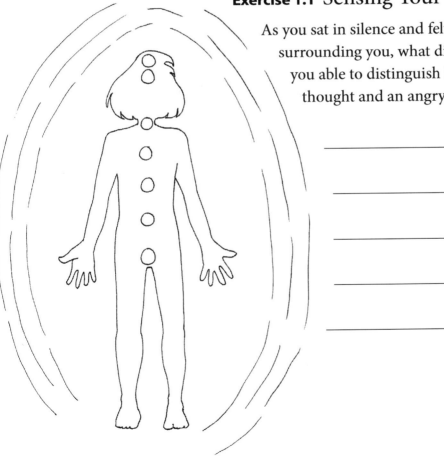

As you sat in silence and felt into this space surrounding you, what did you feel? Were you able to distinguish between a peaceful thought and an angry thought?

_____

_____

_____

_____

It's always wise to start a journey with a destination in mind. What would you like to uncover during our time together?

Exercise 1.2 Seeing and Feeling Energies

Did you feel the energy in your room change while talking on the phone with your friend? Do you think we exchange energy with others in every conversation and interaction? Why?

_____

_____

_____

_____

Exercise 1.3 The Grounding Cord

- Connect a hollow tube of energy from your hips to the center of the earth.

- Intend for foreign energy to leave your aura and drain down to the earth.

- Be aware. Visualize/imagine this happening.

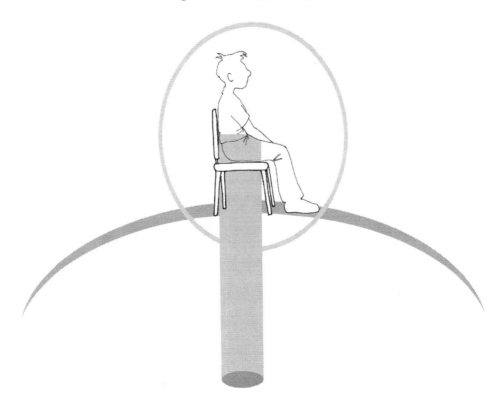

Have you ever walked into a room and felt leftover energy? Have you ever sent an "energy bomb" of unkind thoughts someone's way? How do you feel about that now?

Exercise 1.4 The Golden Sun—Calling Back our Life Force

- Imagine a gold ball of energy above your head. Place a giant magnet in the middle of that sun.

- Intend for all your scattered energies (your life force) to zoom back into that sun.

- Have the sun clean up this energy so it's in alignment with you.

- Add other qualities you would like (for instance: relaxation, peace, joy).

- Pop the sun and fill your body and aura with life force energy.

Write about what you felt as you did Exercises 1.3 and 1.4.

Did you find that you could feel the grounding cord as it attached to your hips? Do you feel it now? What about the golden sun? Did you feel the scattered parts of you zoom back into the sun? (The first time I did this exercise I was surprised at the amount of my energy that I had left scattered in past conversations and future projects.)

Draw or write about your aura. What colors do you imagine are most dominant? What do those colors mean to you?

Exercise 1.5 Grounding Meditation

I use this meditation every morning to set my space, to feel grounded, and to fill in with my own life-force energy. Write about your experience.

_____

_____

_____

Your Final Thoughts on Chapter 1   The Energy of Should

Removing foreign energy and filling in ourselves with our own life force will help to quell our inner critic. We'll explore this more in the next chapter, but first, write about who is the voice of "should" in your life. Is this the dominant voice of your inner critic?

_____

_____

_____

_____

Sit in stillness every day; allow time to think, to feel, to be. As you come to know yourself, you will be able to differentiate your own true wisdom from the constant chatter of your inner critic.

What might your highest self be telling you right now?

CHAPTER 2 Releasing Negative Self-Talk

Big Picture Ideas

- The Inner Critic is the story of who others think we are:
    - Our parents' hopes and dreams for us
    - Neighbors' judgments about what children should say and do
    - Society's rules and regulations about how we should behave
- All of these judgments and "shoulds" are mashed together, and they drown out our own true wisdom.
- You can learn not to listen to these judgments. What came in can go out!

Exercise 2.1 Who Do You Think You Are? (The Name Web)

This exercise will help bring into focus the internal dialog of who you think you are. On the next page, fill in your name web. Reflect upon what you like most about being you. Think of some of your mother's favorite phrases she used in describing you, phrases your inner critic bombards you with, or what your best friend would say about you.

Draw your name web in the space below. It might look like this: a spider web of words and associative feeling-states.

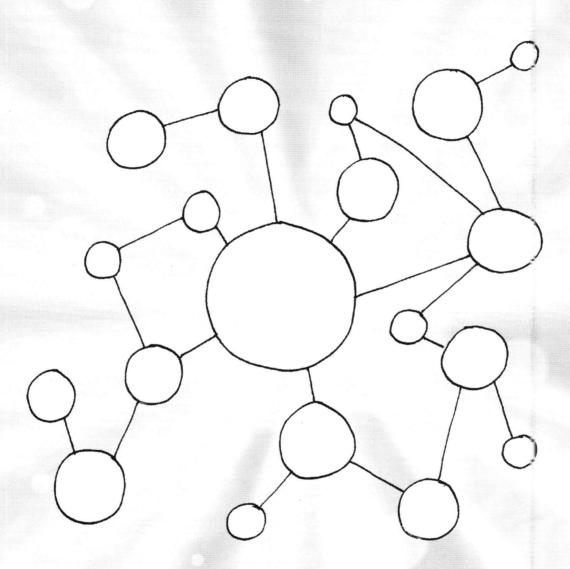

Exercise 2.2 Whose Voice Is That?

As you worked with a phrase from your name web, write about whose voice you found occupying your thoughts and what it felt like to allow this voice to leave your body and aura by way of your grounding cord.

_____

_____

_____

More on Exercise 2.2 Donna's Experience

In chapter 2, I discussed how Donna's mother taught her a "get along at all costs" attitude. To release that attitude, Donna let the words, "Don't rock the boat," slide out of her body and land on the floor. Choose one of the phrases from your name web and have some fun picturing it as a gooey ball of foreign energy as it moves down to the floor. What did it look like? Energy moves when we bring some humor and lightness into our awareness. Think of this exercise as a game of Squish the Funky Goo. Go ahead: stomp on it!

_____

_____

_____

Giving your inner critic a name such as Annoying Alan or Angry Alice brings an added lightness to this very heavy energy.

What name might fit your inner critic? Draw or write about your inner critic.

Exercise 2.3 Tapping for Wellbeing

Tapping the spots on your body called "meridian points" (shown below) is a very powerful tool for emotional and physical wellbeing. Don't worry too much about tapping in a specific order, just tap and tell your story. Tap away until you feel a shift in your body. If the story you're telling morphs into a completely different tale, that's OK. Just go with it and see what happens.

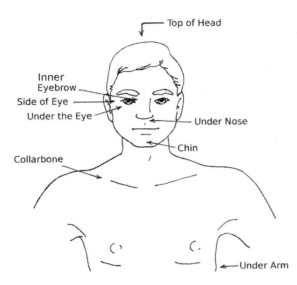

Rate your feeling-state before and after tapping on a scale of 1 to 10, with 10 being the highest:

Beginning _____ Ending _____

What story did you say while you were tapping?

_____

_____

_____

_____

_____

As you clear away a lower vibrational energy by tapping—which sends the energy down your grounding cord—and as you shrug off or stomp on that energy, you defuse the power of a story you've been telling yourself. As you do so, you allow space in your aura for energies that are in alignment with who you truly are. So be sure and use the golden sun to fill yourself in with your own life-force energy. Nurture yourself. Be kind to yourself. Love yourself.

Write about your experiences with tapping. What stories would you like to work on next?

Exercise 2.4 Blowing Up a Rose

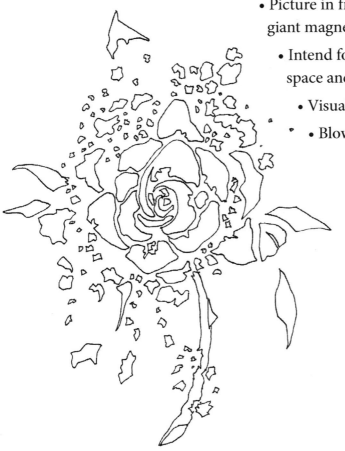

- Picture in front of you a rose that contains a giant magnet.
  - Intend for foreign energy to leave your space and go into the rose.
    - Visualize it happening.
    - Blow up that rose.

Write about your experience with blowing up a rose.

_____

_____

_____

_____

_____

P.S. This is my all-time favorite tool. I use it every day to remove the energy of others from my space.

In Exercise 2.4, Blowing Up a Rose, you may have noticed that the energy being drawn out of your body and into the rose was full of color. Each energy vibrates at a set frequency, and we see that frequency as a certain color or mixture of colors.

How do you see anger?

What color is joy for you? What about peace? Responsibility?

Begin to build your energy vocabulary and write down the associations here. Throughout the rest of our journey together, we will use this technique to decipher the energy of the feeling-state behind the story.

Chapter 2 Key Concept

Energy moves as we become aware of it. Bringing your awareness to something you want to release is the first step. Then, from a place of ease, not effort, intend for it to move out. And watch in amazement as it does!

Write about your thoughts after reading chapter 2. What energies have you already let go? Our inner critic is multilayered. First pick the low-lying fruit, the easy energies. Then, as you gain confidence in using the tools, move on to releasing the more difficult stories.

_____

_____

_____

_____

As we think so we become. Who do you want to become?

Bringing in the Positive

Big Picture Ideas

- Thoughts and feelings are extremely powerful.

- A universal truth is this: like attracts like.

- As you think and feel you will be.

Exercise 3.1 Your Heart Traits

List your best qualities—don't be shy—write them down!

_____

_____

_____

_____

Think of your daily meditation as your special treat to yourself. Quiet and solitude allow you to connect with your own true wisdom.

How hard is it to allow time for yourself? Are you so busy tending to everyone else's needs that you don't take time to value your own? What does that say about how you view yourself? Are you worthy?

Exercise 3.2 Mirror Exercise

This is one of the most powerful exercises in *Tame Your Inner Critic*. Write about what you felt as you stood in front of the mirror and read your list of heart traits aloud. (You might want to come back to this exercise when you're working in chapter 11 to see if your experience is different).

"It's easy to live for others, everybody does.
I call on you to live for yourself."

—RALPH WALDO EMERSON

Can you live for yourself? Will you put yourself first?

Remember what the flight attendant always says, "Put your own oxygen mask on first before you help someone else."

Write about how you live for others and write about how you live for yourself. Compare the two. Are you in balance or out of balance?

Exercise 3.3 Coming into Alignment

In the space below write out each of your heart traits. If you find that your actions are not in alignment with your heart trait, then describe an action you will take to bring yourself back into alignment.

Heart Trait #1 _____

Coming into Alignment

_____

_____

Heart Trait #2 _____

Coming into Alignment

_____

_____

Heart Trait #3 _____

Coming into Alignment

_____

_____

*"When you are content to be simply yourself
and don't compare or compete, everyone will respect you."*

—Lao Tsu

Are you comfortable in your own skin, doing your own thing, living your own life? Or are you looking outside of yourself for validation and approval?

Heart Trait #4 _____

Coming into Alignment

_____

_____

Heart Trait #5 _____

Coming into Alignment

_____

_____

Heart Trait #6 _____

Coming into Alignment

_____

_____

How hard is it to admire all parts of you?

Exercise 3.4 Your Statement of Being

Write it here:

_____

_____

_____

_____

_____

Extra space to write about whatever comes up for you right now:

Chapter 3 Key Concept:

Our primary purpose in life is to remember who we really are and to live our life with this purpose in mind.

Write about your thoughts after reading chapter 3.

_____

_____

_____

_____

*"We must be willing to let go of the life we planned,
so as to have the life that is waiting for us."*

—JOSEPH CAMPBELL

What's waiting for you?

Your Tree of Life

Big Picture Ideas

- Your tree of life is a metaphor for how you express your uniqueness to the world. Is your tree full of your own hopes, dreams, and wisdom? Or is your tree full of other peoples' "shoulds" and other peoples' hopes and dreams?

- Simplifying your life allows you time to hear your own true wisdom.

- Saying "no" is not easy. Open up your throat to speak your mind. Stand tall in your own truth.

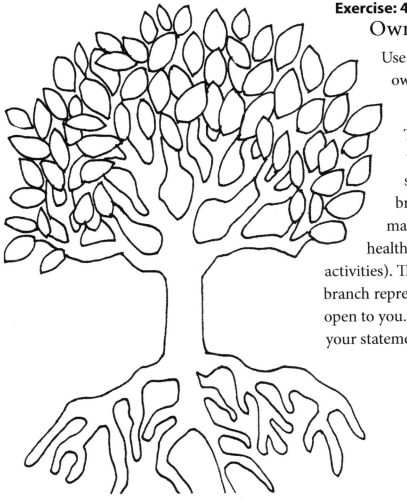

Exercise: 4.1 Draw Your Own Tree of Life

Use the next page to create your own tree of life.

The trunk represents your soul essence, your statement of being. Each branch is an activity or a main part of your life (your health, your job, your outside activities). The fruit hanging from each branch represents the choices that are open to you. Below your tree write out your statement of being.

Draw your tree of life.

More on **Exercise 4.1** Your Tree of Life

Branch 1 – My Health How does the state of your health square with your statement of being? Example: If kindness is one of your heart traits and also part of your statement of being, how kind are you to your body? How judgmental are you of people who you view as not being kind to their own bodies? Write out a plan of action below, including ways to bring your health into alignment with your statement of being. (Look back over Exercise 3.4 and write out your action plan below.)

_____

_____

Branch 2 – My Job List the main activities of your job. Are these activities in alignment with your statement of being? If not, how might you remedy the situation? We make choices every day; maybe there's a choice you can make that tips the workload to be more in alignment with your joy.

_____

_____

Branch 3 – My Outside Activities List your main outside activities and again think about how you might bring them into alignment with your statement of being.

_____

_____

Are you feeling some resistance to making changes? That's a normal reaction, but you have tools to blow up that energy, run it down your grounding cord, or tap it out of your system.

Remember: you get to choose. No one is forcing you to change, but think of how you'll feel once your inner critic is calm and your actions are in alignment with your joy.

Exercise 4.2 Seeing Energies

Write about what you experienced as you visualized the energy of a situation. The first time I ever visualized a soap bubble in front of my closed eyes and understood that I was able to change the energetics of the situation through my intention, I was filled with awe and wonder. Write about what you felt.

_____

_____

_____

_____

_____

Exercise 4.3 Picturing Your Dream Life

What are the labels you've chosen for your manila envelopes?

_____

_____

_____

_____

More space for **Exercise 4.3**

Jot down the web addresses with images that you want to snip or quotes that you find on social media sites.

CHAPTER 4 KEY CONCEPT:

Consider all that you've accomplished so far and write about how you think of yourself today. Then check back on the name web you drew in chapter 2. Acknowledge how much baggage you've already released.

Write about your thoughts after reading chapter 4.

_____

_____

_____

_____

_____

_____

Saying "no" is not easy, especially for women or men who were raised to be "nice." Does that sound familiar in your own life?

Chakras and Your Life Force

Big Picture Ideas

- Chakras are the energetic way stations linking our Spirit to our physical body.

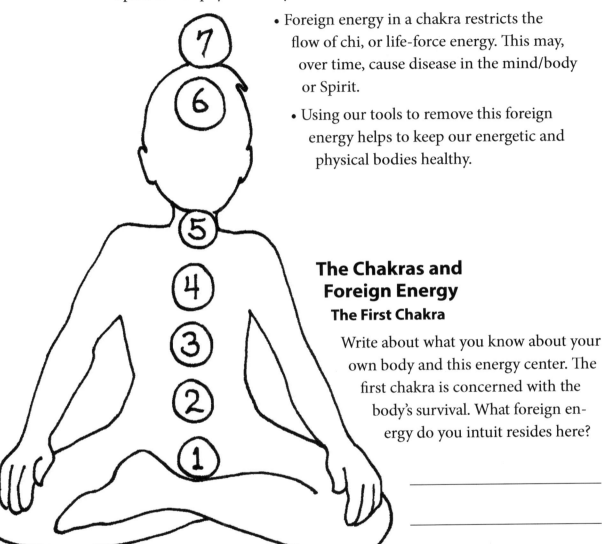

- Foreign energy in a chakra restricts the flow of chi, or life-force energy. This may, over time, cause disease in the mind/body or Spirit.

- Using our tools to remove this foreign energy helps to keep our energetic and physical bodies healthy.

The Chakras and Foreign Energy
The First Chakra

Write about what you know about your own body and this energy center. The first chakra is concerned with the body's survival. What foreign energy do you intuit resides here?

_____

_____

_____

_____

_____

The adrenals are associated with the first chakra. In our overly stressed lives, it's not uncommon for us to experience adrenal fatigue. Is this you? Write or draw what you notice regarding stress, work, and busy-ness.

The Second Chakra

This chakra is your emotional center. If the second chakra is full of "should" energy, then you may not be comfortable fully expressing your emotions. Is this true for you? What foreign energy (other peoples' thoughts of how you should express emotion) resides here?

_____

_____

_____

The Third Chakra

This chakra is your power center. It's the seat of your willpower, your drive, your "gumption," and your "get up and go." Who's in this space? (Hint: if you are a perfectionist, consider who might have controlled you at one time in your life).

_____

_____

_____

The pancreas is the endocrine gland associated with the third chakra. Do you reach for sweets to give you an energy boost? If so, then think of filling in with a golden sun first. See if that is the energy boost you really need.

What boosts your level of energy? A certain person? A certain place?

Write about what drains you of energy. A certain person? A certain place? Or event?

What action steps might you take to nourish your power center, your third chakra?

The Fourth Chakra

This is your seat of self-worth. Much of the work we are doing in our journey together centers around being as kind and compassionate to yourself as you are to others. Write about what you feel right now about being you.

_____

_____

_____

Do you leak energy out to other people in an effort to be accepted or well-liked?

_____

_____

_____

This is very illuminating – if you're up for it.

For a day, record your inner dialog. Start with what you think about as you first awaken in the morning. Write about what you feel about your body as you get ready in the morning. Jot down your thoughts about how you view yourself as you go about your work day. Are you hiding parts of your personality? Why?

The Fifth Chakra

This is your communication center. Whose energy is occupying this space? Your own energy or someone else's? Write about a time when your throat felt dry, tight, and full of cotton. What were you not able to express?

_____

_____

_____

Exercise 5.1: Clearing Your Throat Chakra

Write about a time when there was something you wanted to communicate, but couldn't. Did you find that clearing your throat in the way described in exercise 5.1 made a difference? What colors did you notice leaving your body? What emotions and feelings do you associate with those colors?

_____

_____

_____

Read your Statement of Being out loud to a friend. Write about how you feel as you declared yourself to your friend, and to the Universe.

The Sixth Chakra

Do you believe that children are more intuitive than adults? Did you have an imaginary playmate when you were young? Do you know someone who can sense when you are in a bad mood?

_____

_____

The endocrine gland associated with your sixth chakra is the pineal gland. This small pine-cone-shaped gland sits right in the middle of the energetic space we call the center of your head. It is often referred to as a "cosmic antenna" that attunes us to the frequencies of clairvoyance and "clear sight." As we work together and clear out the center of our head, we also attune the pineal gland to new and higher vibrational frequencies.

Close your eyes and imagine yourself in the center of your head. Imagine that right behind you is this very small pine-cone-shaped structure called the pineal gland. Imagine it vibrating at a clear, grass-green color. (The frequency of grass-green allows for clear sight and higher levels of clairvoyance.)

Draw a picture of how you see yourself sitting in the center of your head. Are you a beam of light, or do you see a miniature version of your body?

When your sixth chakra is open, you see the world as it is, without judgment. Are you judgmental? A little? A lot?

The Seventh Chakra

Your seventh chakra is all about how you want to be seen by the world. Is there a mismatch in how you think of yourself and how you want others to think of you? How comfortable are you with being you?

_____

_____

_____

Earth and Cosmic Energies

Earth energy comes up through the soles of your feet and cascades out the back of your first chakra.

Write about what you feel as that energy courses through the bottom half of your body.

Cosmic energy comes in at the top of your head then moves down the back and into the first chakra. There it mixes with the earth energy. The two energies then rise up the front of your body and out the top of your head, then down your arms and out the palms of your hands.

Do you feel the mixture of earth and cosmic energies coming up the front of your body? What sensations do you experience as the mixture spouts out the top of your head?

_____

_____

_____

_____

_____

_____

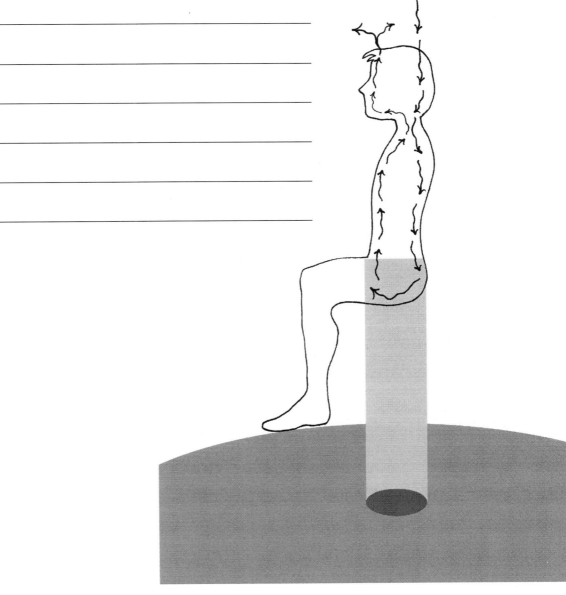

"People are like stained-glass windows.
They sparkle and shine when the sun is out,
but when the darkness sets in,
their true beauty is revealed only if there is light from within."

—Elisabeth Kübler-Ross

As we remove the stories and the baggage from our space, we shine. Do you have a friend who shines from the inside? Describe or doodle that person, and remember that you shine too!

Exercise 5.2: Mother Earth and Father Sky Meditation

After listening to the meditation, record your experience here

_____

_____

_____

CHAPTER 5 KEY CONCEPT:

We have both a physical and an energetic body. They "talk" to each other by exchanging energy through the chakras and the endocrine glands. When we hold tension in our chakras (a story of how things should be, emotional baggage about what should have happened and didn't, or thoughts and feelings of how we should be), that tension can cause disease or upset at the physical level over time.

Write about your thoughts after reading chapter 5. Have you experienced this correlation between energetic dis-ease and a disease of the body?

_____

_____

_____

_____

Being in effort keeps energy stuck where it is. Bring some lightness and amusement to your day. Intend for foreign energy to leave your system without a need to replay the event or circumstance. Keep the drama-queen energy at bay.

Write about how you've moved out a heavy energy using one of your tools (tapping, blowing up a rose, grounding). What happened as you brought some lightness to the exercise?

CHAPTER 6 The Energy of Relationships

Big Picture Ideas

- We unconsciously exchange energy with people all the time.

- Your inner critic is a mash-up of the thoughts, feelings, and judgments other people have sent your way and that you've accepted into your space.

- With all this foreign energy in your space, it's hard to decipher what's your own true wisdom and what's not.

- By using the tools—grounding cord, golden sun, blowing up a rose, tapping—we are removing other peoples' energies from our space.

- This allows us to hear more of our own true wisdom.

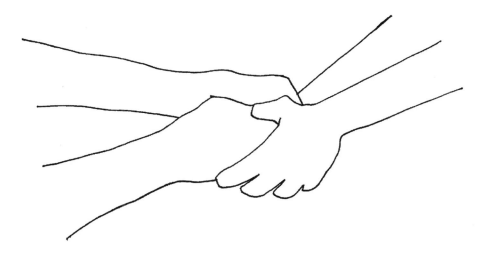

Exercise 6.1 Creating Your Protection Bubble

Your protection bubble is as unique as you are. Sometimes I use a platinum coating; other times I see wire mesh. Every day as part of your morning meditation, intend for this protection bubble to surround your aura, preventing foreign energy from entering your space.

What's your protection bubble look like? Describe or draw it below.

Exercise 6.2 Finding Your Space between Stimulus and Response

What was your body's response to doing this exercise? How did it feel when you tore those pieces of paper to shreds or hit the delete button? Does your body feel different now? Why do you think that is the case?

_____

_____

You've been developing a library of your own feeling-states and their associative colors. What's the energy of joy feel like?

_____

What about anger? _____

Peace? _____

What color is your place of employment? _____

What color is your home? _____

Here's more space for you to write about other feeling-states and their associative colors.

_____

_____

_____

You have a choice every day regarding the attitude you will embrace. Write about a time that you found the nanosecond between stimulus and response and that you consciously chose your reaction.

Exercise 6.3 Setting the Space

Exercise 6.3 is an interesting exercise. What was your experience with setting the space before a difficult conversation? Did you feel your protection bubble in place? Did you consciously open your throat chakra beforehand?

Write about your thoughts after reading chapter 6 on relationships.

You cannot change events that are happening to you, nor can you change the other person. The only thing you can do is change how you react. Difficult, but not impossible.

What do you think?

CHAPTER 7 Shine Bright: Understanding Your Mirrors

Big Picture Ideas

- Everything in our lives is an outward reflection of how we think and feel on the inside.

- Several tools (grounding cord, golden sun, blowing up roses, tapping) help to move foreign energy out of your body and aura, making room for your own true wisdom to shine.

By becoming conscious of a belief we hold, we can change the vibration of it. In *Tame Your Inner Critic,* I gave the example of one of my beliefs, "I should go to the gym." Then I explained how I changed the vibration by getting rid of the "should" statement and rephrasing it to be: "Exercise is good for my health." Write down one of your own beliefs that you would like to consciously change.

_____

_____

_____

_____

*"Each relationship you have with another person
reflects the relationship you have with yourself."*

—ALICE DEVILLE

Think back to the beginning of our work together. Reflect on how the relationship
you have with yourself has changed since that time. Write or draw your thoughts.

Exercise 7.1: Your Template—Your Fourth Chakra

After you came out of the meditation offered in exercise 7.1, and after you've read your statement of being aloud, write about how you felt.

_____

_____

Exercise 7.2: Our Most Important Mirrors

List the top five people who are your major mirrors and the traits that have influenced your life.

1 _____

2 _____

3 _____

4 _____

5 _____

What are the common threads? Why have these people had a major impact on your self-image?

_____

_____

"There are two ways of spreading light:
to be the candle or the mirror that reflects it."

—EDITH WHARTON

Write about the memories and emotions this quotation brings up for you:

When were you the candle that spread light?

When were you the mirror that reflected the light that someone else carried?

Are you comfortable being both?

Are you ready to update your thoughts and feelings around these major influencers, or are you stuck reliving past hurts? Is your lesson complete, or do you have more to learn from each person?

_____

_____

Exercise 7.3 Understanding an Over-the-Top Emotion

What emotional triggers do you face? Do you see an overarching theme developing between the people in exercise 7.2 and an experience from exercise 7.3?

_____

_____

Exercise 7.4 Meditation—Looking through the Mirror of Love

Write about what you felt as you imagined the bubble filled with your best energies and colors.

_____

_____

_____

_____

_____

Spend some time reflecting on the how your childhood experiences have promoted your growth. Record some of your memories on this page.

Chapter 7 Key Concept:

Every event, person, and experience in our life is a mirror reflecting back to us a lesson, challenge, or feeling-state that we have chosen to experience. Life really is a mirror; do you like what you see?

_____

_____

_____

Energy flows between family members even if you are not physically together. What energy would you like to send to one of your major mirrors?

_____

_____

_____

Write about your thoughts after reading chapter 7.

_____

_____

_____

Write about what you think your overarching life theme might be.

PART 1 Recap: Taming Your Inner Critic

As we pause for a moment at the end of part 1, look over
your name web from chapter 2. Have you cleared some of
this foreign energy out of your aura?

_____

_____

_____

_____

Revisit the mirror exercise (exercise 3.2). Write about what you felt this time.

_____

_____

_____

_____

Before we move on, spend some time reviewing your progress. What's your inner critic like now? If it's not completely under control, how would you say it's different? What's your next step in calming this voice of judgment or criticism?

CHAPTER 8

Living on Purpose
Key 1: Havingness

Big Picture Ideas

- Havingness is our ability to accept all parts of our life while wanting more at the same time.

- Being in gratitude for all aspects of your life, even the not-so-great parts, means you are coming from a space of abundance, not lack.

Exercise 8.1: Your Resistance to Current Circumstances

List the top five things that are bothersome in your current life:

1. _____

2. _____

3. _____

4. _____

5. _____

If you are not happy with things just the way they are, right now, without exception, why not?

Is there a choice you can make to bring yourself into alignment?

List below what you are grateful for *today*—not yesterday, not last week, but right now, this minute.

_____

_____

_____

Grace

Being content with what you have, right here and right now, is not as easy as it sounds. Write out what you are not grateful for in your life.

_____

_____

_____

What tools will you use to remove some of those feelings of lack?

_____

_____

_____

"Be content with what you have;
rejoice in the way things are.
When you realize that nothing is lacking,
the whole world belongs to you."

—LAO TZU

Contemplate this quote from Lao Tzu, and record your responses:

Exercise 8.2 Be, Do, Have

Make a list of twenty things that you want to be, do, or have:

1. _____

2. _____

3. _____

4. _____

5. _____

6. _____

7. _____

8. _____

9. _____

10. _____

11. _____

12. _____

13. _____

14. _____

15. _____

16. _____

17. _____

18. _____

19. _____

20. _____

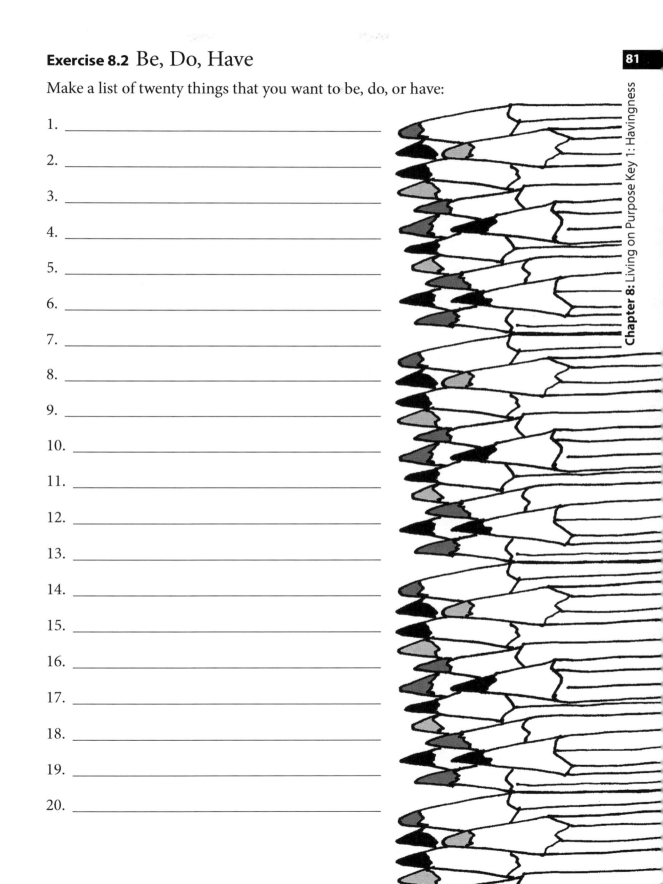

As you sat in meditation from exercise 8.2, what came to mind about your ability to have your selected item? Write about it here:

Exercise 8.3 Removing "Wanter's Block"

Following the sequence in exercise 8.3, list the steps on your ladder:

1. _____

2. _____

3. _____

4. _____

5. _____

6. _____

7. _____

8. _____

9. _____

10. _____

11. _____

12. _____

Write about what you felt as you did this meditation.

_____

_____

_____

You really can change the trajectory of your life by changing the way you think.

If it helps you in any way, the example in the book of wanting a home in Hawaii is my own personal journey. And yes, as of this writing, I'm able to spend my winters on the island of Maui! I tell you this because it really does work.

Write about what "wanter's block" you are ready to tackle next.

Living on Purpose Key 2: The Energy of Money

Big Picture Ideas

- Money is energy.

- It flows in and out of our lives, like the ebb and flow of the ocean.

- Energy (all forms of energy) can be altered. We are not stuck living a life full of stories of how we "should" be. We can change it up by using our tools to move out the energy of others that's mucking up our own sense of who we are. This applies to the energy of money as well!

Exercise 9.1

Create a Name Web for Your Money Life

Draw your money web here:

Write about any surprising associations on your money web. Can you identify the person or event that put that energy into your space? What do you want to do about it?

Exercise **9.2** The Money Timeline Tool

Draw out your money timeline from birth to your current age, making tick marks every seven years along the way.

Write about what money meant to you at 7 years of age, 14 years, and so on.

_____

_____

_____

_____

Is money really the root of all evil?

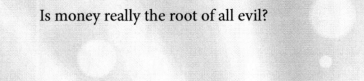

Exercise 9.3 The One Million Dollar Test

Write about how you would spend a million dollars. Then see how high you can go before you hit your "set point."

_____

_____

_____

_____

_____

Money is one hot topic! Where are your blocks to having money? Were you raised to believe that there wasn't enough to go around?

Exercise 9.4 Moving Your Money Energy

After reading or listening to this meditation, write about what you felt as your money energy left your first chakra.

_____

_____

_____

Your Money's Home

What would it be like to live by the principle, "How you treat money is the way money will treat you"?

_____

_____

_____

Creating Your Own Money Story

What's your new money story? Write it here:

_____

_____

_____

Paying money forward is a great way to keep the circulation going.

What are some thoughts that come to mind about how you might do this?

Exercise 9.5 Setting Your Money Bubble

Describe your money bubble below:

_____

_____

_____

_____

_____

_____

_____

Final Thoughts on Chapter 9

Write any other beliefs or ideas you have about money now that you have finished working in chapter 9:

_____

_____

_____

_____

Money Havingness is all about your emotions, thoughts, and feelings about money. Can you have money? How much money can you have? Can you have lots and lots? Is there a cap on your havingness when it comes to money?

CHAPTER 10

Living on Purpose Key 3: Manifesting

Big Picture Ideas

- When you create something, you always create its energetic form first as a thought or idea.

- This energetic blueprint turns into a physical item, calling like energies together in a four-step process: getting clear on what you want, being able to "have it," requesting it, and then waiting in certainty.

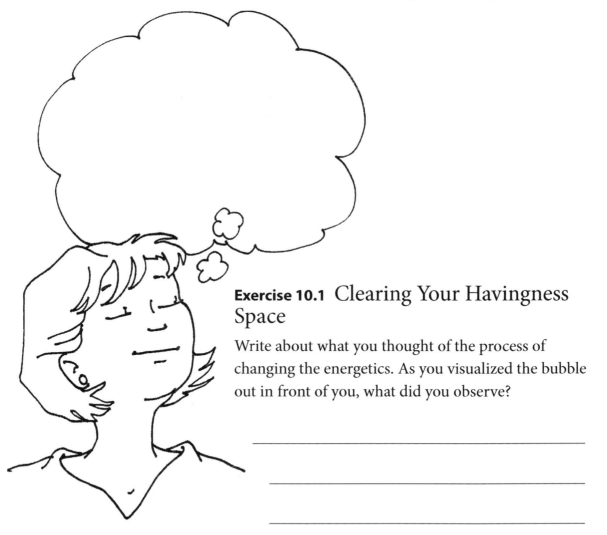

Exercise 10.1 Clearing Your Havingness Space

Write about what you thought of the process of changing the energetics. As you visualized the bubble out in front of you, what did you observe?

_____

_____

_____

_____

You can change a belief at any time by consciously choosing a new belief. Catch yourself in the process of thinking or saying a "should" statement such as "I should go to the gym today."

Consciously think about how you might change that belief around. Write your "should" statements and their turn-arounds in the space below.

Becoming Clear on What You Want

It's the multiple requests we send out that get in the way of manifesting our desires. Write out a desire, being as specific as you can about what you want.

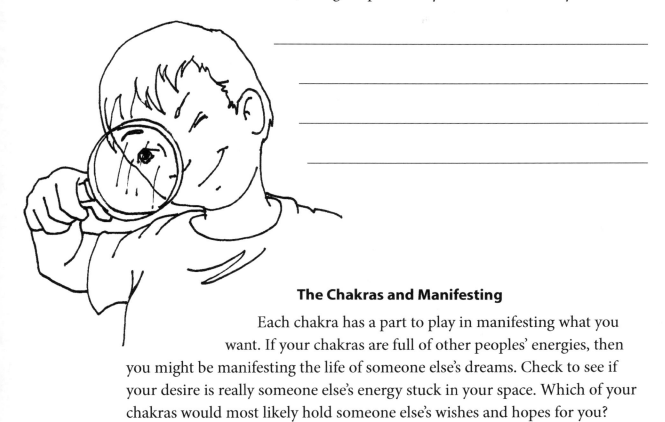

_____

_____

_____

_____

The Chakras and Manifesting

Each chakra has a part to play in manifesting what you want. If your chakras are full of other peoples' energies, then you might be manifesting the life of someone else's dreams. Check to see if your desire is really someone else's energy stuck in your space. Which of your chakras would most likely hold someone else's wishes and hopes for you?

_____

_____

_____

Craving and striving are some of the more difficult energies to clear. Check to see if you are grasping after your desired outcome.

Write about it, and also write about how you used some of the tools to clear that striving energy. Did you blow up a rose? Tap on it?

Exercise 10.2 Creating a Mock-Up

Write out your desire and the process of mocking it up.

_____

_____

_____

_____

_____

Napoleon Hill, author of *Think and Grow Rich,* is credited with saying, "Our minds become magnetized with the dominating thoughts we hold in our minds and these magnets attract to us the forces, the people, the circumstances of life that harmonize with the nature of our dominating thoughts."

What are your dominating thoughts like today? Are they different from the dominating thoughts you had in the beginning of this journey of discovery?

Write out the helpful hints for doing a mock-up.

_____

_____

_____

Parking Karma

Do you know someone with great parking karma? What about other types of "good luck" like always getting the best seats in the house, or selling a home at the highest price? Why do you suppose this person/people have all the luck?

GOOD
PARKING
KARMA
ONLY

_____

_____

Final Thoughts on Chapter 10

_____

_____

Keeping a list of your mock-ups prevents you from unconsciously sending out two mock ups for the same thing. In the space below write out the date and a description of each of your mock-ups.

CHAPTER 11

Living on Purpose Key 3: Waiting in Certainty

Big Picture Ideas

- Waiting in certainty is living in the present moment.
- It's being in the center of your head, experiencing life as it is—right here, right now.

Exercise 11.1 Mindfulness Experience

Mindfulness is a skill, like learning to ride a bike. Were you able to stay focused, feeling into your body and sensing your body and Spirit aligned?

_____

_____

_____

Mindfulness is being aware of what is happening without wishing it were different. How much of your time do you spend wishing and hoping that life were different?

Exercise 11.2 Five Minutes of Mindfulness

Record your experience as you took this five-minute mindfulness break.

_____

_____

_____

_____

_____

Exercise 11.3 Deflecting Anger and Judgment

Write about your experience of standing in nonjudgment. Were you able to sense the other person's emotional state yet remain detached? Did you throw any judgment energy back in their direction? If so, don't beat yourself up, just be in amusement and consider what you might do differently next time.

_____

_____

_____

Are you living life without regret? If not, what do you regret and why? Do the tapping tool on the story and move out the invalidation and expectation energy that is keeping you stuck in regret.

Forgiveness: For Giving Space

Mindfulness is learning to accept yourself and others exactly as they are with compassion and grace. As you release all judgments and expectations, you enter the vibration of forgiveness: for giving space. Are you extra hard on yourself? Do you need to give yourself more space?

_____

_____

_____

Exercise 11.4 The Blue Room Meditation of Forgiveness

Write about your experience with the Blue Room Meditation:

_____

_____

_____

Final Thoughts on Chapter 11

_____

_____

_____

Before we move on to the last chapter, let's check back in with your inner critic. What's your internal dialog like these days? Have you begun to hear the whispers of your highest and best self?

CHAPTER 12 Discovering Your True North

Big Picture Ideas

- Our inner critic's voice is a mash-up of all the "shoulds," the criticisms, and the judgments that other people have sent our way and that we've accepted as our own truth.

- Thoughts travel and are sticky. But what sticks to you can be removed by using some of the energy tools such as grounding, tapping, and blowing up a rose.

Exercise 12.1

Listing Your "Shoulds"

List your life purpose "shoulds". Have you been told that your life purpose is to be happy, to find a job of passion, to heal those around you, to leave a legacy, to have children? List them here:

1._____

2._____

3._____

4._____

5._____

6._____

7._____

8._____

9._____

10._____

11. _____

12. _____

13. _____

14. _____

15. _____

16. _____

17. _____

18. _____

19. _____

20. _____

21. _____

22. _____

23. _____

24. _____

25. _____

26. _____

27. _____

28. _____

29. _____

30. _____

31. _____

32. _____

33. _____

34. _____

35. _____

36. _____

37. _____

38. _____

39. _____

40. _____

41. _____

42. _____

43. _____

44. _____

45. _____

46. _____

47. _____

48. _____

49. _____

50. _____

51. _____

52. _____

53. _____

54. _____

55. _____

56. _____

57. _____

58. _____

59. _____

60. _____

61. _____

62. _____

63. _____

64. _____

65. _____

66. _____

67. _____

68. _____

69. _____

70. _____

71. _____

72. _____

73. _____

74. _____

75. _____

76. _____

77. _____

78. _____

79. _____

80. _____

81. _____

82. _____

83. _____

84. _____

85. _____

86. _____

87. _____

88. _____

89. _____

90. _____

91. _____

92. _____

93. _____

94. _____

95. _____

96. _____

97. _____

98. _____

99. _____

100. _____

Whew! That's one long list of shoulds. Now go back through the list circling common themes. Are you trying to please a certain person? Who? What energy tool would help clear that energy?

Exercise 12.2
Finding Clues to Your Uniqueness

Write about what joy means to you, or draw the picture of joy:

Exercise 12.3 Learning Joy from the Child You Were

Write or draw what your seven-year-old self told you about joy.

Reflect upon how far you've come on this journey of discovery. Go back and look at your name web from chapter 2. Write about what you've discovered about yourself.

Exercise 12.4 Review Your Journey

Pull out the positive phrases from your name web and write them here:

_____

_____

Write out the adjectives from your statement of being that best describe you:

_____

_____

Review your tree of life and describe the choices that bring you joy:

_____

_____

Write out what you learned from the One Million Dollar test:

_____

_____

What are you doing when time stands still for you?

_____

_____

More Writing Room:

Write about joy, write about purpose, write about who you are now, write about your inner critic's voice, write about how you view the world now.

Exercise 12.5 A Treasure Map of Joy

It's now time to open up your manila envelopes from exercise 4.3. There's room on the next page to make some notes on how you would like to create your vision board. After your board is complete, I would love for you to take a picture of it and email me at *della@dellatemple.com*. I will post reader vision boards on my website and on my blog.

What ideas do you have on creating your vision board?

Exercise 12.6 Finding Your Unique Gift

What is your unique gift and how will you share it with the world?

_____

_____

_____

_____

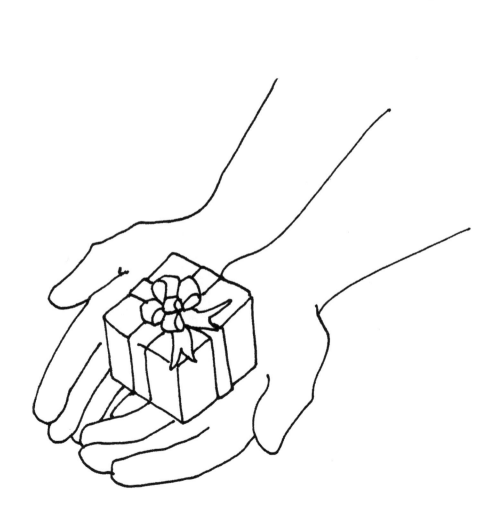

Before we close please take a moment to write your thoughts about the next steps you will take on your journey of discovery. What's different now?

The Next Phase

I hope you've enjoyed our time together and learned to validate the wonderfully exquisite being that you are. Living a life on purpose means that you are filled with joy and enthusiasm. You know your life's purpose deep within your core, and you gladly share this gift with others.

We are all connected. As you raise your frequency to match your unique purpose, you raise the vibration of the thoughts and feelings you transmit into the world. Think of that. As you think and feel joy and love and enthusiasm, those thought-forms travel from you to others around you. As other people pick up those vibrations, they will begin to match that higher vibration. Like attracts like. Your thoughts are beacons of knowingness, calling back to you events and circumstances that allow you to shine bright and stand tall.

That is Grace.

Following your purpose in the deepest sense means that you are not concerned with the shoulds of the world. It is not about what you do that is important; it is about the attitude and feelings you bring to what you do. When your thoughts, feelings, beliefs, words, and actions support your life's purpose, you are in grace. That is the joy. As you come to know, deep within your soul, that you are living a life full of inner purpose and meaning, you radiate this joy out into the world, affecting everyone around you.

You are here on earth to discover your Higher Self, your Spirit, and to listen to your own internal wisdom. As you do this, you understand that your true mission in life is to express your unique gift—and to share it with the world.

Cheers,
DELLA

Resources and Suggestions for Further Study

If you have enjoyed our work together and would like to continue into a deeper and more profound acceptance of yourself and others, then I suggest looking into the following programs and books. First and foremost:

Boulder Psychic Institute in Boulder, Colorado

http://boulderpsychicinstitute.org/

Choose your thoughts. Choose your emotions. Choose your life. Boulder Psychic Institute is a spiritual sanctuary for individuals seeking truth, freedom, and peace in this lifetime. Director and founder Miwa Mack teaches students to open up to their own psychic abilities in an atmosphere of ease, fun, and nonjudgment. There is nothing "woo-woo" about this program. It is a down-to-earth, easy-to-understand guide to opening up your own psychic abilities. I am a graduate of this program, and under Miwa's guidance and tutelage I have tamed my inner critic and I am living my life on purpose. I shine bright because of the work I have done at the Boulder Psychic Institute. Thanks Miwa! Tele-classes allow students from all over the world to participate.

Psychic Horizons in Boulder, Colorado

www.psychichorizonscenter.org

Cofounder and codirector Mary Bell Nyman and codirector Hope Hewetson have said that people attracted to classes at Psychic Horizons Center know that energy is real and they want to learn to work with it. Students learn to access their inner wisdom and use it to create their own reality by taking charge of their experiences. I have studied at Psychic Horizons as well, and I have found this program to be full of playfulness and awareness. As Mary Bell says, "Energy is not fussy." Learn to open to your clairvoyance from a space of fun and ease.

Books to Speed You on Your Journey of Discovery

The Subtle Body: An Encyclopedia of Your Energetic Anatomy by Cyndi Dale (Sounds True, 2009).
A comprehensive, fully illustrated reference book of the human energy system. I was astounded at the information housed in this one volume. A must-read for anyone interested in the world of energy awareness.

You Are Psychic: The Art of Clairvoyant Reading & Healing by Debra Lynne Katz (Llewellyn Publications, 2004).
Ms. Katz utilizes the same tools I do—grounding, golden sun, blowing up roses—but takes readers a step further on the journey of discovering their own true nature. This practical guide is easy to follow and perfect for anyone interested in developing or strengthening their psychic abilities.

The Energy of Money: A Spiritual Guide to Financial and Personal Fulfillment by Maria Nemeth, Ph.D. (Ballentine Publishing Group, 1997).
Full of exercises and how-to's, Dr. Nemeth explores the tool called money and how to harness its energy to fulfill your life's dreams.

The Soul of Money: Transforming Your Relationship with Money and Life by Lynne Twist (W.W. Norton and Company, 2003).
The author delves into the soulful purpose that money can play in your life and how prosperity and abundance are represented by more than just our material possessions.

Your Soul's Plan: Discovering the Real Meaning of the Life You Planned Before You Were Born by Robert Schwartz (Frog Books, 2007).
If you are skeptical but interested in reincarnation, this is a great place to start. Through case studies, Mr. Schwartz follows four trance mediums as they work with clients to uncover the reasons they face the life challenges that they do.

The Not So Big Life: Making Room for What Really Matters by Sarah Susanka (Random House, 2007).
If you are ready to de-clutter and move to a more simple way of living, you will enjoy Susanka's exercises, which are designed to help you remodel your life to fit who-you-are-right-now.

Energy Medicine: Balancing Your Body's Energies for Optimal Health, Joy, and Vitality by Donna Eden with David Feinstein, Ph.D. (Jeremy P. Tarcher, 1998). This easy-to-follow illustrated guide to energy medicine is another must-have book.

More Recommended Readings

Loving What Is: Four Questions That Can Change Your Life by Byron Katie with Stephen Mitchell (Three Rivers Press, 2002).

Wherever You Go, There You Are: Mindfulness Meditation in Everyday Life by Jon Kabat-Zinn (Hyperion, 1994). The quintessential guide to mindfulness.

A Life of Being, Having, and Doing Enough by Wayne Muller (Random House, 2010).

Getting into the Vortex: Guided Meditations CD and User Guide by Esther and Jerry Hicks, the Teachings of Abraham (Hay House, 2010).

Conversations with God: An Uncommon Dialogue—Books 1, 2, and 3 by Neale Donald Walsch (G.P. Putnam's Sons, 1996).

About the Author

Della Temple has a bachelor's degree in business administration/accounting and a master's degree in organizational leadership (string theory for business nerds). She combines her love of anything analytical with her wide-ranging interest in quantum physics and the world of energetic healing. She is a certified Reiki Master and has studied clairvoyance and psychic healing at Boulder Psychic Institute under the direction of Miwa Mack. She believes that being psychic is a very natural state of being. It is a skill, just like playing the piano or singing on key. It takes a teacher, a willingness on the part of the student to be receptive to new ideas, and some time spent in practice. In her book, *Tame Your Inner Critic: Find Peace and Contentment to Live Your Life on Purpose,* Della invites the reader to experience opening to their own intuition on the journey toward discovering their life's purpose.

Della is currently writing her second book, *Conscious Grieving: Spiritual Tools to Help You Navigate the Loss of a Loved One,* about her experiences after her son Rick's death four years ago. She lives with her husband in the mountains above Boulder, Colorado, and stays on the island of Maui every winter. Visit Della's website at *www.DellaTemple.com* or follow her at *DellaTempleAuthor* on Facebook.

Made in the USA
San Bernardino, CA
15 September 2017